CYCLICAL NATURE OF DOMESTIC VIOLENCE

Table of Contents

CHAPTER 1

THE Cyclical Nature of Domestic Violence (global)

"Women in violent relationship often leave their batterers only to cycle back into the relationship".

This book brings an awareness of the impact of domestic violence to children. I chose this topic because I have always been interested in this field. More specifically, it became relevant to my practice in my second placement year in a school where I worked with Looking after a Child who had witnessed domestic violence, and I observed the impact it had on her development.

A further interest in this topic derives from my current placement in a private fostering agency where many cases from Safeguarding Teams in different Local Authorities are domestic violence related. This gave me an insight into some of the impact domestic violence can have upon a family. Working with the affected children and families highlighted for me, in a very direct way the lack of knowledge regarding the impact domestic violence can have on children, and this was especially evident in behavioural issues presented by children who had been affected. These concerns called for a need to look at how well equipped I was to efficiently execute a practice that would address these issues and minimise the impact.

Consequently, working with the affected children and families also enabled me to observe first-hand, how professionals in various settings respond to domestic violence issues. I was then able to evaluate the strength and shortcomings with regards to how the needs of the affected children and families were addressed.

Every Child Matters (Department of Children Schools and Families 2003)' and the subsequent Children Act passed in November 2004 raised the degree of accountability, especially at Local Authority level. Therefore, understanding of domestic violence, cycles of abuse and its impact is necessary in order to plan an intervention to minimise the suffering of victims as an informed practitioner.

I hope to apply the expertise gained in this book to real world situations and to develop skills in problem identification and analysis through my book.

How does domestic violence start?

According to Spivak, (2014), CDC reports that one every 5 women and one in 7 men experience domestic abuse in their intimate relationships. In places like US, intimate violence accounts for upto15% of domestic violence cases. There are certain risk factors that are known to promote domestic violence (Hanmer,2013). These are the factors that must be observed when trying to ascertain the inception of domestic violence.

In a normal relationship it is very difficult to ascertain the extent of domestic violence being experienced by individuals and the risk factors serve as a benchmark for determining this.

Risk Factors to Domestic violence

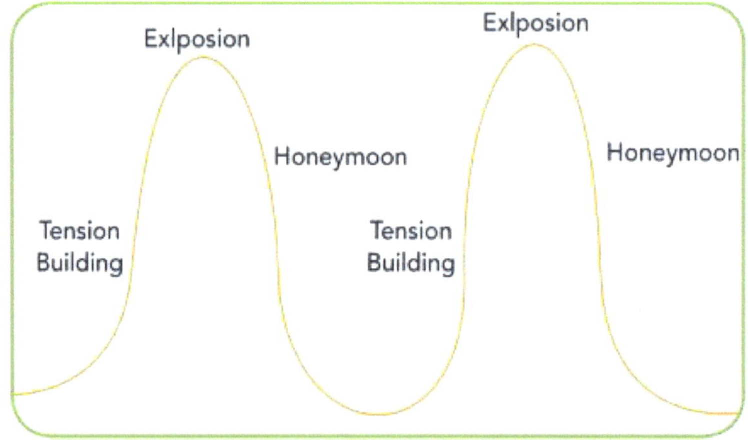

Cyclical Nature of domestic violence

According to Snyder, (2022), teenagers manifesting aggressive behavior could be a risk factor that there is an extent of domestic violence going on in his or her environment. Personality traits that are antisocial also a risk factor to domestic violence. Emotional insecurity is also a risk factor because most of the time it results in intimate relationship fights because of jealousy and other insecurities.

History of depression and suicide attempts is also a risk factor, mental instability. Belief in rigid gender roles and hostility towards women is big risk factor that promotes domestic violence. Desire for control or power in relationships is another risk factors as it promotes authoritarianism which promotes violence between partners. Economic stress and illiteracy are a risk factors because the knowledge of dealing with domestic circumstances in missing and therefore one acts in a violent manner. Lack of friends and social isolation is correlated with high likelihood of committing domestic violence acts. Poor problem-solving skills and impulsivity is also a risk factor to domestic violence (James,2013).

Therefore, the early signs of domestic violence are related to the risk factors, and they originate from these factors as well. Certain relationship factors also contribute to high risk. Relationships that are marred with incidences of insecurity, dominance and past divorce attempts are full of unanswered questions which raise eyebrows and are likely to translate to violence in the long run.

According to Dutton, (2011), at society level, there are certain cultures which heighten gender expectations that men should be dominant in relationships and women should be submissive all the time. At the community level some of the risk factors include high crime rate, poverty, increased levels of unemployment, illiteracy. All these combined are likely to lead to domestic violence. CDC asserts that children who have grown up in toxic relationships which consists of a lot of relationship violence are likely to fall into the same trap and maybe become worse than their predecessors. Therefore, when the risk factors are monitored and controlled well, then the cases of domestic violence will reduce gradually. To curb instances of domestic violence, it is important to work on the underlying issues that trigger domestic violence (García-Moreno,2013).

Warning Signs of Domestic Violence

Richards, (2017) asserts that domestic violence exists in 3 categories: physical abuse, sexual abuse, and psychological aggression. The warning signs highlighted below will be a sure sign of impending domestic violence.

Intimate relationships are normally built on a foundation of privacy and confidentiality. Therefore, it is difficult to establish if someone is being abused or not. The risk factors might be available, but it might not necessarily mean that there is an incidence of domestic violence. Domestic violence affects people of all walks of life and therefore you should be careful not to blame the victim. However, there are red flags that signify that the relationship is not having a positive outlook.

Alcohol or substance abuse is likely to be a red flag for domestic violence (Synder,2022). In most cases people take alcohol for entertainment but when binge drinking sets in, it is an outward manifest of bigger problem lying in the inside. It is likely to lead to domestic violence because alcohol impairs judgement and daily drinking leads to violence. Alcohol is linked to violent cases especially domestic violence. Alcohol is also liked to risky behaviors like sexual encounters with unknown partners and this is likely to lead to relationship fights and insecurities.

Relationship insecurities are warning signs for domestic violence (Synder,2022). If one person in the relationship starts accusing the other of flirting and infidelity negative energy builds up which is privy to violence. A relationship that is full of insecurities has a lot of negative energy caused by feelings of betrayal and mistrust and this unhealthy environment is likely to lead to cases of domestic violence.

Financial abuse is where one partner in a relationship controls all the money related resources in the family. This leads to lack of money for the other partner to get what he or she needs.

These people always call for accountability for every penny they issue. According to a recent study 99% of the cases of financial abuse result in domestic violence. This is because one partner bullies the other and this leads to rebellion then violence erupts (Reeves,2010).

Verbal abuse and threat of violence is the most common sign of domestic violence. According to CDC, 75% of cases of physical domestic violence are always alluded to certain threats and ill words used beforehand (Culpeper, 2011). Therefore, as one says so he or she does. A threat pf violence always results from premeditated thoughts of domestic violence. Therefore, this is a sign of domestic violence that one ought to observe. When someone talks ill of the partner especially to outsiders, it is a first sign of looming domestic violence. It is because of the buildup of relationship issues overtime and the same negative energy if not dealt with sooner and is taken to the family setting, it's likely to result in instances of domestic violence.

Extreme sensitivity to any little emotional distress is also a sign of domestic violence. This is because of previous experiences and therefore a partner might be in emotional turmoil.

Increased reaction to a little emotional issue characterized by impulsivity and outburst is a sign of emotional instability and distress. This means that there could be underlying emotional issues that the partners are facing. Mood swings and episodes of intense anger always result from this emotional distress. Love bombing is also a sign of looming domestic violence (Synder,2022).

Definition of Domestic Violence

The term domestic violence comprises of disproportion of power where an abuser employs intimidation and hurtful actions to dominate their victim.

People who have a relationship with another even if it's with a person met online, romantic partner, family member for example, brother or a sister, children, young people, faces the danger of domestic violence.

This issue is common across various parts of the world, impacting both men and women. However, a significant majority of victims are women. In the United States, one in three women is reported to have experienced some form of domestic violence from an intimate partner. Domestic violence can encompass anything from verbal abuse to severe injuries, which tragically, in some cases, can lead to fatalities. Despite healthcare professionals being able to identify domestic violence and offer safety referrals, it remains a substantial public health concern, predominantly affecting women and often remaining unreported, leaving the possibility for recurrence.

Domestic violence typically takes place within the personal sphere of the affected individual, whether through a romantic partner, former partner, or family member. The most prevalent forms of domestic violence include sexual abuse, physical abuse, economic exploitation, and psychological manipulation (John, 2022).

Physical abuse involves deliberately using force to cause physical harm to a victim, potentially leading to manslaughter. Conversely, sexual abuse encompasses using force during a sexual act without consent, which is illegal. Economic abuse entails actions like destroying property or limiting access to shared finances, thereby curtailing a victim's economic autonomy. Psychological abuse can manifest as harassment, coercion, or defamation (John, 2022).

Different forms of violence can occur separately or simultaneously, depending on the characteristics of the abuser. In many cultures, and even in certain parts of mainstream society, domestic violence is sadly accepted as a societal norm, particularly when women are the victims.

In my opinion, this normalization of domestic violence is alarming. Often, when victims report these incidents, authorities either take minimal action or ignore the issue altogether. Domestic violence stems from various factors such as social and economic status, religious beliefs, and the educational background of those involved. Additionally, situations that affect emotions and individual sensitivity can negatively impact the domestic environment, leading to conflicts between partners.

For example, during the COVID-19 pandemic, heightened tensions within households resulted in an increase in domestic violence cases.

Research indicates that COVID-19 imposed significant stress on families, individuals, and communities, affecting both their economic stability and health. Measures like social distancing resulted in some women experiencing domestic violence through neglect and exploitation (Malik & Naeem, 2020).

This surge in domestic violence can be viewed as a consequence of the pandemic, receiving minimal attention for evaluation and resolution on a community or national level. Often, secondary issues like these are not considered a priority for policy reforms. Nevertheless, given the extensive impact, it's crucial to raise awareness about domestic violence—its characteristics, repercussions, and strategies for avoidance and prevention.

Outsiders often downplay the seriousness of domestic violence because they don't grasp the cycle it follows and how it operates. For example, it's simple for observers to suggest that leaving is the obvious choice once violence occurs. However, leaving is not easy, mainly due to the pattern of abuse. This cycle consists of three stages: the tension-building phase, the crisis phase, and the honeymoon phase. The tension phase is when the victim senses an impending crisis (John, 2022).

During the crisis phase, there are threats, destruction, and an eruption often accompanied by alcohol or drug abuse.

(Shelter for Help in Emergency, 2023)

The honeymoon phase involves the abuser making promises to change, expressing love, and assuring the victim that the violence won't happen again. However, the reality is that victims of domestic violence typically leave and return to their abusers at least seven times. Moreover, when action isn't taken on domestic violence cases, it escalates their frequency and severity.

Domestic violence inflicts various impacts on victims, affecting them physically and psychologically. Furthermore, it detrimentally influences a victim's self-esteem and productivity.

Beyond its personal toll, domestic violence has wider implications for national healthcare. In the United States alone, around 10 million people are impacted by domestic violence annually (Huecker et al., 2022).

Various studies on domestic violence delve into different aspects, examining its impact on children, the influencing factors behind its occurrence, and various other issues.

However, the central focus remains on raising awareness about the severity of the problem and establishing support systems for victims. Additionally, it involves identifying abusers and connecting them with counselling services to tackle the underlying causes (Huecker et al., 2022).

Numerous indicators of domestic violence include mental health disorders, exposure to abuse during childhood, a mindset accepting violence as permissible, and being a victim of abuse in early life. Abusers can benefit from understanding their actions and being encouraged to recognise and address the triggers leading to violent behaviour (Huecker et al., 2022).

A collaborative approach involving teams or communities can effectively tackle the problem of domestic violence. It's crucial for all stakeholders within society to recognise and fulfil their roles in creating a support system for victims. For example, religious leaders can provide compassion and guidance to victims, aiding them in making informed decisions to navigate their circumstances.

Research highlights that a team-based, inter-professional care model assists victims in assessing, reporting, and handling their encounters with abusers (Huecker et al., 2022).

Raising awareness about domestic violence begins with recognising the indicators that signify one might be experiencing abuse. In many cases, victims are unaware that early signs of abuse could evolve into more severe situations, making it challenging to break free from the abuser.

Various signs to be vigilant about include increased displays of anger, threats of physical harm, discussions of violent intentions, more frequent physical altercations, and a rise in alcohol or drug consumption. Being mindful of these indicators can empower potential victims to distance themselves early on, preventing the normalization of abusive experiences (Huecker et al., 2022).

Despite society often downplaying domestic violence as a minor issue needing little attention, statistics reveal its alarming growth as a public health concern. Victims and witnesses often refrain from reporting such incidents, allowing the problem to persist and impact large populations.

The urgency of the situation calls for continued public awareness about the various forms, causes, signs, and effects of domestic violence in our society. Additionally, research suggests a collaborative approach involving healthcare professionals and religious leaders to offer support, information, and empathy to victims of domestic violence.

Regarding men as victims of domestic violence, it is defined as a pattern of abusive conduct within any relationship, where one partner uses it to assert control over their intimate partner.

There are various forms of domestic violence, such as physical abuse, where force is used against the victim. Sexual abuse occurs when the abuser coerces the victim into sexual acts without consent. Emotional abuse undermines the victim's sense of self-worth, while economic abuse makes the victim financially dependent. Psychological abuse instils fear through intimidation, threatening what the victim cherishes most, among other forms. Although domestic violence is often associated with men as perpetrators and women as victims, it's essential to acknowledge that men can also be victims.

Research in sociology over the past twenty-five years, notably by leading experts like Kelly, consistently indicates that both men and women commit violence at similar rates (Kelly, 792). Understanding men as victims of domestic violence is best approached through sociological Feminist theory and Agenda-setting theory.

In a literature review, Susan Lawrence, an Emergency Nurse Practitioner, explores the factors contributing to domestic violence and why men who experience it often hesitate to report or acknowledge their troubled relationships. Society and the media largely overlook domestic violence, typically portraying women as the sole victims and neglecting violence against men (Lawrence, 2003).

A case study involved a man of short stature, ectomorph body type, and a low socioeconomic background. He sought medical attention for shoulder pain, revealing that his wife had struck him, but no further action was taken. During the conversation with the nurse, he avoided eye contact and appeared withdrawn. The nurse, noted as Box 1 in the case study, observed a lack of available resources to support the client.

The nurse had a private room for the examination and confidential discussion with the client.

Several months later, the same client returned with physical injuries and disclosed past and ongoing issues, including testicular pain caused by his wife's abuse throughout their marriage. Despite this, he resisted any intervention between them. The client seemed relieved to confide in the nurse confidentially but expressed a reluctance to leave the marriage.

The nurse felt a sense of achievement in working independently and creating an environment where the client could openly discuss his experiences without facing judgement. This open conversation became a crucial way for this man to navigate his pain caused by domestic violence. While support systems are readily available for women and children, there's a lack of suggested support for male victims of domestic violence. The courts and society often cling to a particular image of victims (Schechter, 1996), where appearance plays a significant role.

Meeting a certain visual criterion of distress or being seen as a battered individual can impact various aspects, including child custody cases, where those perceived as helpless might lose custody solely based on this portrayal.

Fitting into this victim image becomes vital as it influences how seriously one's situation is handled and whether they are believed or not. Ximena E. Mejia notes the limited availability of therapy specifically tailored for men. One crucial aspect highlighted is that due to societal conditioning, men often suppress coping mechanisms necessary for dealing with trauma. Therapy needs to assist men in redefining masculinity, thereby enhancing and fortifying their coping skills.

The initial phase of therapy involves stressing a redefined masculinity, fostering hope, resilience, and transcendence. Following this, effective therapy moves into a phase where the trauma and its lasting impacts can be addressed.

The women's movement acted as a driving force in empowering women to take charge of their own lives.

As the feminist movement progressed, feminist theory emerged and started to influence fields like psychology and counselling (Mejia, 2005). Society tends to place more weight on men when it comes to issues of violence and subsequent trauma. Maxwell E. Mccombs and Donald L. Shaw introduced the agenda-setting theory, suggesting that mass media significantly shapes public perception by framing topics for discussion. While the media doesn't dictate what to think, it does shape what people should think about. Michael Howlett further refines this theory to establish a more contemporary understanding (Soroka, 1999).

Feminist theory has evolved over time, altering its significance. Sociological feminist theory examines gender inequality and how it structures our social world. Adopting a feminist perspective involves delving into comprehending these gender inequalities.

For years, right from birth, babies are raised differently based on their gender. Lise Eliot, author of "Pink Brain, Blue Brain:

How Small Differences Grow into Troublesome Gaps - and What We Can Do About It," shared with Helena de Bertodano of the Times of London that, in reality, the brains of boys and girls aren't significantly dissimilar. It's the societal conditioning they encounter that leads them to adopt and internalise gender-specific roles. These ideas about what girls should do or boys shouldn't cry are instilled through various channels like family, schools, media, and peers. Social learning also plays a role through observation.

Children swiftly start displaying gender-stereotyped behaviours by the age of two, which influences their lives as they grow. Evaluating domestic violence victims through a feminist lens suggests that due to these ingrained gender stereotypes, it's challenging to envision men as victims of domestic violence. People generally don't perceive men as capable of being victims or targets of abuse. Instead, they are associated more with moral and physical strength, seen as protectors of the household.

This concept doesn't quite fit with the notion of someone being degraded or mistreated.

When men do seek assistance, they often feel their masculinity is undermined—a barrier that women haven't faced as extensively (Smith, 2018). This aligns with feminist theory, as gender norms can hinder individuals from living freely. Men shouldn't fear seeking help because it's perceived as a sign of weakness.

Men tend to conceal their struggles due to the fear of judgment, uncertainty about where to seek help, fear of exacerbating the situation, or not being believed (Lawrence, 2003). Their lesser emotional expression compared to women can lead to emotional build-up, psychological issues, and even suicide.

Women, being perceived as more sensitive, are often seen as victims. Gender expectations should not influence court treatment; crimes should be addressed impartially without considering stereotypical gender roles. Gender should not dictate people's actions or experiences.

However, a weakness of feminist theory lies in its constant evolution and roots in patriarchal values.

Patriarchy, a societal structure where men hold more power than women, may overlook discussing male victims in LGBTQ relationships. Queer theory opposes restrictive ideas and emphasises the value of diversity.

Queer theory challenges established ideas about sex and gender. In situations involving two men, it questions the essence of patriarchy as it removes the female element.

Within discussions around heterosexual relationships, members of the LGBTQ community are often overlooked. According to NCADV, in a study focusing on male same-sex relationships, only 26% of men sought police assistance after experiencing severe violence. This is significant because domestic violence can occur in any relationship, and limitations in feminist theory might impact how such situations are managed.

Feminist theory is evolving in society but has not fully adapted to current societal norms. The agenda-setting theory suggests that media can influence public opinions by selecting certain news stories, thereby shaping what people think about.

Searching for information on men as victims of domestic violence yields limited results. This topic is often treated as taboo or even joked about. As highlighted by Lawrence and Mejia, there's an issue with the available resources for male victims.

While there are women's shelters and the Violence Against Women Act (1990), similar services are not available for men. Addressing this begins with raising awareness and openly discussing the topic, even if it contradicts established beliefs. While it's unacceptable for men to perpetrate violence, it's equally important not to dismiss them as victims.

The scarce portrayal of men as victims of domestic violence leaves them feeling isolated and disregarded, believing their situation isn't significant if it's not being openly discussed. Media coverage on this issue, particularly following the Me-Too movement, has been minimal, leaving men to deal with their issues alone.

Men who gather the courage to speak out often encounter ridicule and unhelpful suggestions like "hit her back" (Smith, 2016).

Media attention unintentionally focuses more on one group over another, leading to an imbalance in articles, news coverage, and popularity. Flaws in the Agenda-Setting Theory arise from people's diverse backgrounds, cultures, and perspectives, causing varied responses to media content.

Domestic violence may not be a significant concern for some individuals. Despite exposure to information through various media channels, people possess the ability to ignore certain topics. Take veganism, for instance, which has gained increased attention in recent years.

Despite numerous sources highlighting its benefits for health and the environment, revealing the realities of meat production, etc., many continue consuming meat due to the convenience or because they don't see the direct impact on themselves.

Essentially, people may dismiss information if it aligns with their personal convenience or beliefs.

Public attention to issues typically follows a cycle where awareness peaks initially but gradually decline (Soroka, 1999). Media outlets constantly seek the next big topic to discuss, contributing to this fluctuation in public attention.

Once a topic emerges, discussions spark, prompting people to contemplate solutions. While some issues become hot topics for a few weeks, others linger for years. Important matters can be side-lined or forgotten as a more popular subject takes precedence, underscoring the significant impact of media on society, yet it's society's responsibility to take action.

If solely left to mass media, issues remain unresolved. It's the courageous individuals who defy media norms and champion what they believe should be discussed. Neglected areas, like gun violence laws, often result in more mass shootings. However, some individuals choose not to wait for the media's agenda but set their own.

Addressing domestic violence against men requires the audience to confront and break the taboo around this issue.

In conclusion, the analysis of men as victims of domestic violence aligns with feminist theory, despite its substantial gap in acknowledging LGBTQ relationships. This theory is continually evolving, allowing it to adapt to societal changes. The portrayal of men as victims through the agenda-setting theory and media reflects gender inequalities in society.

Societal stereotypes of men contribute to the lack of visibility of this issue. Tackling the problem directly appears to be the most logical approach. It's essential for society to begin dismantling the gender expectations ingrained in our culture.

Men experience emotions and have every right to express them, just as women do. Normalising these emotions from a young age is crucial. Suppressing feelings is detrimental to mental and physical health. Bottling up emotions can lead to more significant problems, so something as simple as discussing feelings can make a significant difference. Reimagining masculinity and advocating for fair treatment of experiences is key.

Recognising that anyone, regardless of their masculinity, can face these challenges is vital. Physical strength does not equate to being too tough to experience issues like domestic violence.

Engaging with one another, exchanging insights, and acknowledging the need for a better world are essential aspects of this shift.

Domestic Violence in Kenya

Causes of Domestic

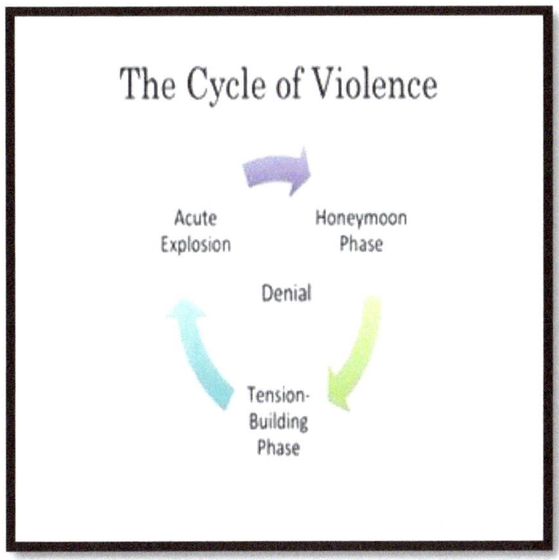

Approximately 40% of married women in Kenya have reported instances of domestic violence (Domestic violence in Kenya - Wikipedia, 2022). Domestic violence in gneral is normally caused by harmful behavior against a partner or family member.

In most cases it can be rape, physical abuse and forced prostitution and most of the time women are most victims, even though there has been an element of male buse. Religion, illiteracy, and socio-economic status are some of the reasons for rise in domestic violence cases amongst women. The gender roles of women contribute to domestic violence cases in some parts of Kenya. Pregnant women are more vulnerable to domestic violence because most of them are likely to be married. The unwanted pregnancies are normally blamed on them, and they end up suffering from this. Domestic violence is prone to sexual coercion and the eventuality of this is sexual abuse amongst young and elderly women. The consequences of domestic violence in include stress, physical injuries, hypertension and even pregnancy loss. The statistics of domestic violence cases in most parts of the country in Kenya is underreported because of shame felt by victims of rape, lack of awareness and even mistrust of health workers (Domestic violence in Kenya - Dibaba, (2022).

According to Dibaba, (2022), 38% of domestic violence murders are normally caused by intimate partners.

Recent statistics show that approximately 41% of women had experienced sexual violence from their intimate partners and 40% reported injuries sustained from sexual abuse (Dibaba,2022). The socio-cultural beliefs in Kenya also account for the number of cases of domestic violence in Kenya. For example, 42% of men still believe that wife beating is acceptable (Domestic violence in Kenya – (Dibaba, (2022).

Sexual Coercion

The 2014 Demographic Survey reported that 1 in every 4 women reported instances of sexual abuse from their partners. Sexual coercion is common in Kenya and other African countries especially with adolescents.

Any case where a n individual is forced to have sex with another person against her will is known as sexual coercion. According to Dibaba, (2022), 11% of men and 21% of women aged between 10 and 24 years experienced sexual coercion in their lives. Only 23% of the women and 22% of the men reported these instances to their close family members. Intimate partner coercion was the most common amongst women. Generally, in the lifetime of Kenyan women, 44% of them reported that since they were kids, they have experienced some form of sexual abuse (Adudans,2011).

Gender Inequality

According to Kassie, (2014), women with low levels of education also have low socio-economic status and are highly likely to be victims of domestic violence. This means that they cannot full fend for themselves and depend on their husbands to be their financial providers. Some men even prohibit their partners from being employed to stay within their control. This leads to financial abuse which causes domestic violence. These women are normally helpless and end dup not reporting these incidences of domestic violence that happen in their lives. The transgressing gender norm also can lead to violence, For example, men do not like women who make independent decisions without involving them. In most instances, if a woman does not complete her chores, she is beaten and if she questions the financial decisions of a man the same happens.

A focus Group discussion study showed that male infidelity is widely accepted in Africa while an attempt by a woman to engage in such acts translate to physical abuse. According to , Dibaba, (2022), a survey conducted on men in Africa, physical abuse was a way of forgiving a woman from her transgressions.

Therefore, men think it is accepted to physically abuse women. Amongst the women who were abused, they claimed that the physical abuse showcased love from the partner. This is the belief system that is causing increased cases of domestic violence across Africa.

Education

The low education levels also contribute to domestic violence. A recent study conducted recently showed that there was a correlation between education level of the respondents and those who believed that it is right to beat a woman. The more educated an individual is in Kenya, the less the justification of domestic violence. The same studies also showed that educated mothers taught their children to evade cases of domestic violence.

Mental and Physical Health

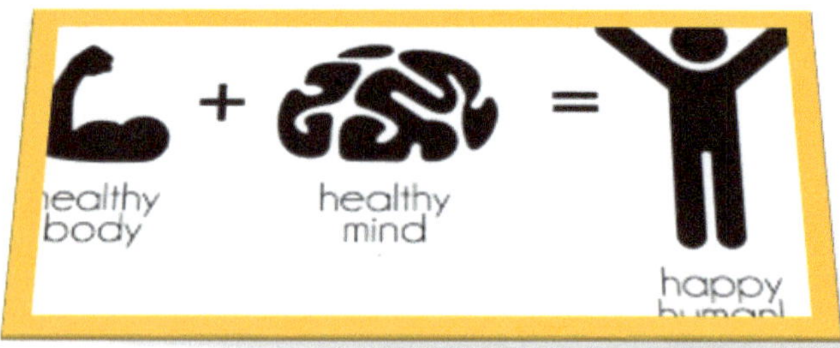

A study by WHO in 2008, revealed that women who reported cases of domestic violence had high probability of developing suicidal thoughts than those who had not experienced violence (Devries,2011). Depression, anxiety, and alcoholism were prevalent amongst the victims of domestic violence. According to a study conducted by WHO in 1998, women who had lifetime PTSD as diagnosis had reported cases of abuse at some point in their life (30.6%). Domestic abuse decreases the dignity and self-worth of most women (Nelson,2016).

Responses to Domestic Violence in Kenya

The effort to curb cases of domestic violence in Kenya has been so gradual. This is attributed to weak institutional capacities and lack of sufficient data because many women prefer not reporting these incidences. Under Sustainable Development Goals (SDGs) Kenya promised to eliminate all kind of sexual violence by 2030 like other counties in Africa (Synder,2022).

In June 2021, Kenya introduced the gender-based violence indicator as a basis of monitoring the cases of gender-based violence in Kenya. Its major function is tracking of gender-based policies and resources deployed to respond and prevent cases of domestic violence.

Kenya has also built gender-based violence recovery centres in all major hospitals to assist victims who have been admitted due to gender-based abuses. Gender desks have also been introduced in police stations to respond to nay cases of violence. Civil Society organizations have been formed and funded to support fight against any gender-based violence. Examples are the Coalition on Violence Against Women and the Federation of Women Lawyers in Kenya. Kenya launched a National Policy on Prevention and Response to Gender Based Violence in 2014 which is a legal document detailing the responses to gender-based violence, the policy framework, and the objectives of fighting gender-based violence in Kenya. The government is currently adopting a multi-agency approach to deal with gender-based violence. This involves the civil organization, UN and the government working collaboratively to end cases of gender-based violence.

The Kenyan constitution also has been used to protect victims of domestic violence through the Kenyan Penal Code. The sexual offences Act provides for how to deal with various kinds of rape. However, the policy document has some loopholes that need to be tightened (Synder,2022)

Impact of domestic violence to children and families

According to Øverlien ,(2010), domestic violence has a snowballing effect on the children as well because when violence erupts, they become victims of the physical abuse. Children who witness the cases of domestic violence are likely to suffer from long term physical and mental health problems. They are prone to anxiety disorder and even depression which is linked to early childhood experience of domestic violence. Children who witness their parents fighting are likely to be violent in future. Children who are in pre-school era can go back to doing things that they used to do when very young including bedwetting and lack of sleep because of fear, anxiety, and terror.

In school going children, domestic violence hurts their relationship with others as they develop low self-esteem. Teens may resort to fighting with family members and truancy sets in. In the long term, the children suffer mental health conditions like depression and anxiety. The impact on women includes STIs, trouble sleeping and minor injuries. Some pregnant women end up losing their unborn babies. The long-term effect on women is PTSD, anxiety, and depression. In cases of death, the children are left orphans with nobody to fend for them. This makes life difficult for most of the children while growing up (Øverlien ,2010).

Comparing domestic violence in UK compared to Africa

According to a Victim Support, (2022) as of March 2020, approximately 5.5% of adults aged between 16 and 74 years experienced domestic violence in 2019-2020 period. This means that 5 in every 100 adults in UK experience domestic violence. However, in Kenya 11% of men and 21% of women aged between 10 and 24 years experienced sexual coercion in their lives.

Only 23% of the women and 22% of the men reported these instances to their close family members. In Kenya, 38% of domestic violence murders are normally caused by intimate partners. In UK, there are numerous forms of domestic violence that is; physical, sexual, financial abuse, emotional abuse, online abuse and forced marriage. In Kenya and Africa at large, the most common forms of domestic violence are sexual coercion and gender-based violence. In Africa, domestic violence is linked to some cultural norms like belief that women must be beaten as punishment for their transgressions.

However, in UK, the life is liberal, women are very educated, know their rights, report cases and initiate lawsuits against their partners.

Therefore, the difference in action points is because of the difference in education levels.

UK provides Independent Domestic Violence Advocates (IDVA), outreach programs and even online assessment for victims. In Kenya for example there is a penal code, but most women live in fear and do not report these cases and are therefore not assisted by the services availed by the government of Kenya.

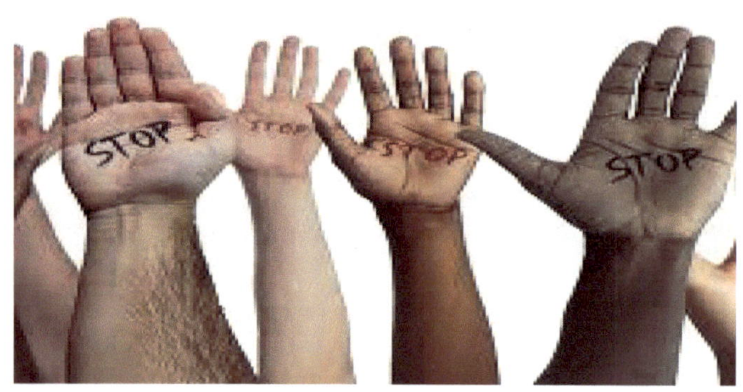

Both counties have active programs but in the UK the programs are well utilized owing to supportive institutional framework compared to Africa. In Africa, the policies and laws have loopholes and the fact that most cases are not reported causes underutilization of the available resources.

In Africa, there are a lot of gender based cultural norms that promote domestic violence. For example, some women believe that being beaten is a show of love while the men believe it's a way of forgiving women from their transgressions. However, in UK the women are empowered and are socio-economically resilient with no backward customs and traditions and this helps to reduce domestic violence cases in UK(Synder,2022).

How domestic violence can be stopped in Africa and UK

Empowering women.

Empowering women involves educating them on the risks of domestic violence and providing for them the avenues of reporting emphasizing on the need to report any looming cases of domestic violence (Kiani,2021). In Africa, more women should be enrolled to school and opportunities created for them to access jobs equally like men. This eliminates the risk of financial abuse. In Africa, empowering women also helps them get rid of the traditional ethnic stereotypes that promote violence like belief in women beating. More stringent regulations should be created for perpetrators of domestic violence to instill fear and create an enabling environment that supports women instead of abusing them. An example is Victim Support UK which has a 10-week program for victims of domestic violence educating them on how to deal with the effects of the violence that they have experienced.

Multi agency Collaboration

There are various interested parties dealing with incidences of domestic violence in both UK and Africa.

A multi-agency approach to deal with gender-based violence should be adopted where all the agencies collaborate by pooling their resources and efforts to achieve the desired synergy (Davies,2021). This involves the civil organization and advocacy groups, UN and the government working collaboratively to end cases of gender-based violence. An example of that in Kenya is the collaboration between the government and the advocacy group.

Increasing Domestic Violence Support Outreach and Support centres

These are outreach programs that support women and men in times of abuse. The outreach programs teach them what to do and how to read signs of domestic violence, the reporting protocols and how they can keep safe to avoid being victims. This can be done through regular campaigns on GBV and domestic violence on the social media and print media. Free workshops and seminars can be set up for people to attend and get more insights on fighting domestic violence. Domestic violence recovery centres should be built in big numbers to accommodate any new cases that are coming up.

An example is Kenya has established the DRC in every major hospital. However, this is insufficient, it should be able to spread across all hospitals including the remote areas.

Policies and Regulations

Tightening loopholes in policies and enacting better laws that are stringent to perpetrators of domestic violence can discourage the incidences of domestic violence because of the sanctions attached to it.

The bible says IN John 20:21 Peace to you, as the father has sent me, I also send you, God has called us to have influence in our world today. There are six examples of heroes in the bible who combined their faith in God with their calling of standing in the gap for OTHERS.

To plan an intervention that would help perpetrators as well as victims in my opinion would be to start a domestic violence intervention business. It could be the best possible solution to get involved in the community as well as making a difference.

To begin with, describing what area of domestic violence the business will cover is essential and what the business entails, what products will be sold, and finally, what the vision is for the business's future.

Pen and paper would be useful at this juncture to jot down an overview of what's the business aim and exactly how everything will be set up, for example, it could be that you're considering starting up a contact centre, mediation and counselling:

The unique selling point would be to provide a centre where family mediation will take place with independent, trained professional helping couples to work out an agreement and a way forward about issues such as arrangements around contact for their children or their finances.

The most important tool to use before domestic violence has taken place and most of the times, there're children caught up in the middle, is Mediation.

Mediation would be easier and less stressful than going to court – and it works. Involving the children makes it easier if their parents co-operate and can help maintain important family relationships.

Parents would usually seek help from friends, family GP, church, referrals could be picked up from the school children attend, play group, interaction with parents in a park etc. At this point, if a referral could be made to an intervention business, mediation could be initiated sooner than later.

Secondly, is counselling. Counselling can be useful for anyone who wants to explore the way they're thinking or feeling further, as well as anyone experiencing a problem or issue, they are keen to resolve. People may choose to speak to a counsellor because they feel they cannot speak to their other half/friends/family about such personal issues, or they may simply wish to speak to a professional with an objective view point.

Thirdly, providing a Child Contact Centre. A Contact Centre is a safe, friendly, and neutral place where children of separated families can spend time with one or both parents and sometimes other family members. They are child-centred environments that provide toys, games and facilities that reflect the diverse needs of children affected by family breakdown.

Forthly,

The next stage would be to outline the product that the business intends to sell. The business will provide excellent quality, affordable, accessible in a supportive safe environment and work in partnership with local authorities and other partner organisations.

It's crucial to outline the sales approach for the product. For instance, we'll market the service through informational packs showcasing our offerings. These pamphlets will be distributed widely, and we'll host events where we'll present our newly acquired marketing materials and details about our services, collecting contacts from potential clients. Additionally, our established business website will promote our childcare services.

It's crucial to follow up with interested parties via phone, email, or letter, arranging comprehensive home visits to delve deeper into their needs and guide them to suitable services. Alongside the support, highlight collaborative services not directly provided by your company and t this point, mentor the charges. If you happen to get referrals from the local authority, they will have their costs covered by them.

What sets this business apart from the competition is the offering of its product/service at a lower price. Additionally, the business distinguishes itself by providing better quality products/services and filling a gap in the market.

Ensure that the aim at this level is to offer top-notch services that are both affordable and easily reachable, focusing on each person's specific requirements. There isn't a universal solution for everyone, so customize every care package to fit the clients' needs, ensuring a supportive and secure environment. Collaboration with parents and families is key to this personalized approach.

Staff and those involved in the business must work alongside a qualified social worker, who will have an insight into the cyclical nature of violence; The business will effectively work toward ending relationship violence.

Interventions will alleviate domestic violence as well as provide mediation services leading to a solution around contact as well as making use of counselling to resolve the impact of domestic violence to its victims and especially children. It is important to have a good understanding of the Children Act (1989) (2004), Fostering Regulations (2011) and 2013 amendments, Every Child Matters (2004) and the Leaving Care Act (2011), as well other legislations and policy documents underpinning the provision of children's services in the UK.

Once all the above have been accomplished, the next step is to describe your background and why this business is suitable, then drafting all the business background detailing the areas that are relevant to this business.

Take account to mention the aims and objectives for running the business, for example, it could be to contribute to the community as well as a place where women and children will be listened to.

Work experience contributes to the success of a successful business enterprise, for example, see a caption of a client named “V” for confidentiality reasons below just to highlight a case scenario that had positive outcomes:

"V" has over 10 years' social care experience within the children and families sector. "V" has a social work qualification with 11 years post qualified experience with fostering and related child protection expertise and I have embarked on a management course. "V" has a good understanding of Violence against Women (2004), Crime and Victims Act (2004) as well as Children Act (1989) (2004), Fostering Regulations (2011) and 2013 amendments, Every Child Matters (2004) and the Leaving Care Act (2011), as well other legislations and policy documents underpinning the provision of children's services in the UK.

Collaborating with local authorities, the business you want to establish will ultimately ensure that all the children and young people in care achieve the five outcomes outlined in the ECM framework. This would ideally be achieved by the company's clear and robust policies including but not restricted to: child protection policy, complaints procedure, safe care policy, equality and diversity, promoting contact and data protection policy as well as our health and safety policy.

We also aim to support healthy eating and exercise, drug awareness, as well as encouraging ways of enjoying and achieving.

Finally, encourage social integration within the community by encouraging children to make a positive contribution, through having children contribute to decision making meetings, as well as for them to aim high so as to achieve economic wellbeing, through a commitment to further education in order to achieve gainful employment.

Giving an example of product and services of what will sell as well as an overview of the day today business operations is important.

The summary of the product or service offered clarifies whether it involves products, services, or a blend of both. It details the fundamental offering and highlights the various available types. Furthermore, it explores the possibility of introducing more products or services down the line.

For example, mentioning that the service will be marketed through informational packs showcasing the available services. These leaflets will be distributed to the general public, and events will be organized where we'll present our newly acquired marketing materials and provide information about our services, while collecting contacts of potential clients.

Additionally, the established having a website will promote the range of childcare services offered. Follow up with interested parties via phone, email, or letter, arranging comprehensive home visits to deeply understand their needs and guide them to suitable services.

The production process or service execution method includes the necessary equipment, tools, intellectual property, or other assets required for the production or delivery of the product/service.

Distribution of leaflets to the public and host events where details about services using recently acquired marketing materials. Contacts of potential clients will be collected. Additionally, the established business website showcases childcare services. Personally, reaching out via phone, email, or letter to those interested, arranging in-depth home visits to explore concerns and guide individuals to suitable services.

The cost to produce/deliver the product(s) or service(s) is being assessed.

The expenses will cover registering the business with Companies House, acquiring office furniture, insurance, rent, and marketing.

The delivery of the product(s) or service(s) will involve various methods, such as home visits, office appointments, or organized family outings and holidays.

There are specific legal requirements essential to initiate this business, including registration with Companies House, compliance with data protection regulations, confidentiality measures, adherence to health and safety regulations, and consideration of intellectual property rights, copyrights, as well as online and distance selling regulations.

The typical customers for the business encompass both individuals and businesses of various ages. The expectation is to attract customers through diverse means such as word-of-mouth recommendations, distributing leaflets to the public, organizing events to introduce the business, utilizing a website to showcase childcare services, and personally following up with interested parties via telephone, email, or letters. The aim is to arrange comprehensive home visits to thoroughly understand their needs and direct them to suitable services.

Several legal requirements are crucial for starting this business, including adherence to the Violence against Women (2004) Act, the Crime and Victims Act (2004), the Health and Safety Act of 1974, the Children Act 1989, and compliance with Every Child Matters (2004) regulation.

It is important to consider the non-asset start-up costs beyond physical necessities for your business.

These encompass expenses such as renting premises, utility bills, production costs, website development, product transportation, business insurance, staff wages, and more. Ensure these costs are accounted for in your Cash Flow Statement Identify businesses that pose competition to your own. Consider similar companies in your area or search online for relevant competitors.

Competitors might include other domestic violence companies or charities.

Customers might choose our business over competitors due to our 24-hour service availability. Additionally, we plan to extend services to Saturdays and Sundays, catering to families unavailable during the week.

The business will be marketed and promoted through various channels such as social media, flyers, word of mouth, newspaper/radio advertisements, and a comprehensive website.

Social media, flyers distribution, use of our marketing table in organised customer focussed events, word of mouth, newspaper/radio advertisement, comprehensive webpage, etc.

If the business faces failure, the immediate plan involves assessing what went wrong, noting the extent of damage, documenting debts and liabilities, and working to rectify the situation. Prioritizing crucial assets like the business team, key employees, and essential documents.

Aiming to learn from the experience and use those lessons to prevent a similar situation in the future. Collaborating with the team, analyse the situation, identify errors, explore solutions, and decide whether to rebuild the existing business or venture into a new opportunity.

If the business encounters difficulty repaying the loan, secure an insurance policy to cover potential loan failure. Additionally, ensure you possess qualifications as a social worker, support worker, foster carer, or childminder, offering alternative avenues to generate income.

REFERENCES

Huecker, M. R., King, K. C., Jordan, G. A., & Smock, W. (2022). *Domestic violence*

John, V. (2022). *Hope When It Hurts: Recognizing the Signs of Domestic Violence* (Doctoral dissertation, Amridge University).

Malik, S., & Naeem, K. (2020). Impact of COVID-19 Pandemic on Women: Health, livelihoods & domestic violence.

Shelter for Help in Emergency. (2023). *Cycle of Violence*. Shelter for Help in Emergency

Adudans, M.K., Montandon, M., Kwena, Z., Bukusi, E.A. and Cohen, C.R., 2011. Prevalence of forced sex and associated factors among women and men in Kisumu, Kenya. African Journal of Reproductive Health, 15(4), pp.87-97.

Culpeper, J., 2011. Impoliteness: Using language to cause offence (Vol. 28). Cambridge University Press.

Davies, P., 2021. Practicing co-produced research: tackling domestic abuse through innovative multi-agency partnership working. Crime prevention and community safety, 23(3), pp.233-251.

Devries, K., Watts, C., Yoshihama, M., Kiss, L., Schraiber, L.B., Deyessa, N., Heise, L., Durand, J., Mbwambo, J., Jansen, H. and Berhane, Y., 2011. Violence against women is strongly associated with suicide attempts: evidence from the WHO multi-country study on women's health and domestic violence against women. Social science & medicine, 73(1), pp.79-86.

Dibaba, Y., 2022. Violence against women in Kenya: data provides a glimpse into a grim situation. [online] The Conversation. Available at: <https://theconversation.com/violence-against-women-in-kenya-data-provides-a-glimpse-into-a-grim-situation-170109> [Accessed 3 April 2022].

Dutton, D.G., 2011. Rethinking domestic violence. Ubc Press.

En.wikipedia.org. 2022. Domestic violence in Kenya - Wikipedia. [online] Available at: <https://en.wikipedia.org/wiki/Domestic_violence_in_Kenya> [Accessed 3 April 2022].

García-Moreno, C., Pallitto, C., Devries, K., Stöckl, H., Watts, C. and Abrahams, N., 2013. Global and regional estimates of violence against women: prevalence and health effects of intimate partner violence and non-partner sexual violence. World Health Organization.

Hanmer, J. and Itzin, C., 2013. Home truths about domestic violence: Feminist influences on policy and practice-A reader. Routledge.

James, L., Brody, D. and Hamilton, Z., 2013. Risk factors for domestic violence during pregnancy: a meta-analytic review. Violence and victims, 28(3), pp.359-380.

Kassie, M., Ndiritu, S.W. and Stage, J., 2014. What determines gender inequality in household food security in Kenya? Application of exogenous switching treatment regression. World development, 56, pp.153-171.

Kiani, Z., Simbar, M., Fakari, F.R., Kazemi, S., Ghasemi, V., Azimi, N., Mokhtariyan, T. and Bazzazian, S., 2021. A systematic review: Empowerment interventions to reduce domestic violence?. Aggression and violent behavior, 58, p.101585.

Nelson, M., Hess, J.M., Isakson, B. and Goodkind, J., 2016. "Seeing the Life": Redefining self-worth and family roles among Iraqi refugee families resettled in the United States. Journal of international migration and integration, 17(3), pp.707-722.

Øverlien, C., 2010. Children exposed to domestic violence: Conclusions from the literature and challenges ahead. Journal of social work, 10(1), pp.80-97.

Reeves, S. and Wysong, J., 2010. Strategies to address financial abuse. Journal of elder abuse & neglect, 22(3-4), pp.328-334.

Richards, T.N., Tillyer, M.S. and Wright, E.M., 2017. Intimate partner violence and the overlap of perpetration and victimization: Considering the influence of physical, sexual, and emotional abuse in childhood. Child abuse & neglect, 67, pp.240-248.

Rivas, C., Ramsay, J., Sadowski, L., Davidson, L. L., Dunnes, D., Eldridge, S., ... & Feder, G. (2016). Advocacy interventions to reduce or eliminate violence and promote the physical and psychosocial well-being of women who experience intimate partner abuse: A systematic review. Campbell Systematic Reviews, 12(1), 1-202.

Spivak, H.R., Jenkins, E.L., VanAudenhove, K., Lee, D., Kelly, M. and Iskander, J., 2014. CDC grand rounds: A public health approach to prevention of intimate partner violence. MMWR. Morbidity and mortality weekly report, 63(2), p.38.

Synder, C., 2022. Understanding Factors and Behaviors That Predict Domestic Violence. [online] Verywell Mind. Available at: <https://www.verywellmind.com/signs-that-a-relationship-could-turn-violent-4100203#toc-risk-factors-for-violence-in-relationships> [Accessed 3 April 2022].

VictimSupport, 2022. Domestic abuse - Victim Support. [online] Victim Support. Available at: <https://www.victimsupport.org.uk/crime-info/types-crime/domestic-abuse/> [Accessed 3 April 2022].

STOP
ABUSE

survivor
issues
social
lawyer
DOMESTIC
ABUSE
abuse

STOP
STOP

NOTE:

NOTE:

NOTE:

NOTE:

NOTE:

NOTE:

NOTE:

NOTE:

NOTE:

www.ingramcontent.com/pod-product-compliance
Lightning Source LLC
LaVergne TN
LVHW052256100826
845147LV00001B/65

* 9 7 8 1 7 3 9 5 3 4 8 0 6 *